Disney

Olaf's FROZEN ADVENTURE

MAD LIBS®

by Mickie Matheis

Mad Libs
An Imprint of Penguin Random Ho...

D1508739

MAD LIBS
Penguin Young Readers Group
An Imprint of Penguin Random House LLC

Mad Libs format copyright © 2017 by Penguin Random House LLC. All rights reserved.

Concept created by Roger Price & Leonard Stern

© 2017 Disney Enterprises, Inc.

Published by Mad Libs,
an imprint of Penguin Random House LLC,
345 Hudson Street, New York, New York 10014.
Printed in the USA.

ISBN 9780515159608
1 3 5 7 9 10 8 6 4 2

MAD LIBS®

INSTRUCTIONS

MAD LIBS® is a game for people who don't like games!
It can be played by one, two, three, four, or forty.

•RIDICULOUSLY SIMPLE DIRECTIONS

In this tablet you will find stories containing blank spaces where words
are left out. One player, the READER, selects one of these stories. The
READER does not tell anyone what the story is about. Instead, he/she asks
the other players, the WRITERS, to give him/her words. These words are
used to fill in the blank spaces in the story.

•TO PLAY

The READER asks each WRITER in turn to call out a word—an adjective or
a noun or whatever the space calls for—and uses them to fill in the blank
spaces in the story. The result is a MAD LIBS® game.

When the READER then reads the completed MAD LIBS® game to the other
players, they will discover that they have written a story that is fantastic,
screamingly funny, shocking, silly, crazy, or just plain dumb—depending
upon which words each WRITER called out.

•EXAMPLE (*Before* and *After*)

" _____ !" he said _____
          EXCLAMATION   ADVERB

as he jumped into his convertible _____ and
                                          NOUN

drove off with his _____ wife.
                              ADJECTIVE

" _____OUCH_____ !" he said _____STUPIDLY_____
          EXCLAMATION   ADVERB

as he jumped into his convertible _____CAT_____ and
                                          NOUN

drove off with his _____BRAVE_____ wife.
                              ADJECTIVE

In case you have forgotten what adjectives, adverbs, nouns, and verbs are, here is a quick review:

An ADJECTIVE describes something or somebody. *Lumpy, soft, ugly, messy,* and *short* are adjectives.

An ADVERB tells how something is done. It modifies a verb and usually ends in "ly." *Modestly, stupidly, greedily,* and *carefully* are adverbs.

A NOUN is the name of a person, place, or thing. *Sidewalk, umbrella, bridle, bathtub,* and *nose* are nouns.

A VERB is an action word. *Run, pitch, jump,* and *swim* are verbs. Put the verbs in past tense if the directions say PAST TENSE. *Ran, pitched, jumped,* and *swam* are verbs in the past tense.

When we ask for A PLACE, we mean any sort of place: a country or city (*Spain, Cleveland*) or a room (*bathroom, kitchen*).

An EXCLAMATION or SILLY WORD is any sort of funny sound, gasp, grunt, or outcry, like *Wow!, Ouch!, Whomp!, Ick!,* and *Gadzooks!*

When we ask for specific words, like a NUMBER, a COLOR, an ANIMAL, or a PART OF THE BODY, we mean a word that is one of those things, like *seven, blue, horse,* or *head.*

When we ask for a PLURAL, it means more than one. For example, *cat* pluralized is *cats.*

MAD LIBS® is fun to play with friends, but you can also play it by yourself! To begin with, DO NOT look at the story on the page below. Fill in the blanks on this page with the words called for. Then, using the words you have selected, fill in the blank spaces in the story.

Now you've created your own hilarious MAD LIBS® game!

ARENDELLE IN WINTER

ADJECTIVE _____

A PLACE _____

A PLACE _____

VERB _____

NUMBER _____

ADJECTIVE _____

SILLY WORD _____

PLURAL NOUN _____

TYPE OF LIQUID _____

PERSON IN ROOM (FEMALE) _____

PART OF THE BODY _____

COLOR _____

NOUN _____

ANIMAL (PLURAL) _____

PLURAL NOUN _____

CELEBRITY _____

VERB _____

MAD LIBS®

ARENDELLE IN WINTER

Come home for the holidays to Arendelle, a winter wonderland as

magically _____ as the North Pole or (the) _____.
                ADJECTIVE   A PLACE

Visitors from as far away as (the) _____ travel to Arendelle to
                                      A PLACE

explore, play, and _____ in this frosty paradise, which becomes
                      VERB

_____ times more breathtaking during the _____
   NUMBER   ADJECTIVE

holidays. Listen for the collective cry of "_____!" from the
                                               SILLY WORD

visiting _____ as they float in ships through the frigid
            PLURAL NOUN

_____ of the harbor and catch their first glimpse of the
TYPE OF LIQUID

stunning winter kingdom. The kind ruler of Arendelle, Queen

_____, has the power to control snow and ice. All it
PERSON IN ROOM (FEMALE)

takes is one wave of her powerful _____ to transform
                                      PART OF THE BODY

her kingdom. Evergreen trees are draped in _____
                                                COLOR

garlands formed from clusters of frosty _____ crystals. Dazzling
                                            NOUN

ice sculptures shaped like flying _____, enchanted
                                     ANIMAL (PLURAL)

_____, and _____ dot the snow-covered
   PLURAL NOUN   CELEBRITY

landscapes. Once you've experienced Arendelle, you'll never want to

_____ anywhere else for the holidays!
   VERB

From OLAF'S FROZEN ADVENTURE MAD LIBS® • © 2017 Disney Enterprises, Inc.
Published by Mad Libs, an imprint of Penguin Random House LLC.

MAD LIBS® is fun to play with friends, but you can also play it by yourself! To begin with, DO NOT look at the story on the page below. Fill in the blanks on this page with the words called for. Then, using the words you have selected, fill in the blank spaces in the story.

Now you've created your own hilarious MAD LIBS® game!

A ROYAL INVITATION

ADJECTIVE _____

PERSON IN ROOM _____

ADVERB _____

NOUN _____

VERB ENDING IN "S" _____

ADJECTIVE _____

CELEBRITY (FEMALE) _____

ADJECTIVE _____

VERB ENDING IN "ING" _____

NUMBER _____

A PLACE _____

NOUN _____

PLURAL NOUN _____

NOUN _____

ADJECTIVE _____

VERB ENDING IN "ING" _____

ADJECTIVE _____

MAD LIBS

A ROYAL INVITATION

Hear ye! Hear ye! By proclamation of Her Royal _____-ness,
<u>ADJECTIVE</u>

Queen Elsa, I—_____, the Royal Crier of Arendelle—do
<u>PERSON IN ROOM</u>

hereby _____ declare that every man, woman, and
<u>ADVERB</u>

_____ who lives and _____ within the
<u>NOUN</u>   <u>VERB ENDING IN "S"</u>

boundaries of this beautiful kingdom is invited to the castle for

a/an _____ holiday party with Queen Elsa and Her Royal
<u>ADJECTIVE</u>

Highness, Princess _____. Please join us in the
<u>CELEBRITY (FEMALE)</u>

_____ courtyard of the castle for caroling and
<u>ADJECTIVE</u>

_____ prior to the Jule Bell ceremony. At precisely
<u>VERB ENDING IN "ING"</u>

_____ o'clock, the official start to the holiday season in our fair
<u>NUMBER</u>

kingdom of (the) _____ will commence with the ringing of
<u>A PLACE</u>

the _____ Bell, just as it has for centuries. Immediately
<u>NOUN</u>

following the ceremony, the queen and princess cordially invite all

_____ in attendance to come inside the _____
<u>PLURAL NOUN</u>   <u>NOUN</u>

walls for a festively _____ lunch followed by dancing and
<u>ADJECTIVE</u>

_____ in the great ballroom. A royally _____
<u>VERB ENDING IN "ING"</u>   <u>ADJECTIVE</u>

time will be had by all!

From OLAF'S FROZEN ADVENTURE MAD LIBS® • © 2017 Disney Enterprises, Inc.
Published by Mad Libs, an imprint of Penguin Random House LLC.

MAD LIBS® is fun to play with friends, but you can also play it by yourself! To begin with, DO NOT look at the story on the page below. Fill in the blanks on this page with the words called for. Then, using the words you have selected, fill in the blank spaces in the story.

Now you've created your own hilarious MAD LIBS® game!

THE FIRST HOLIDAY IN FOREVER

ADJECTIVE _____

PLURAL NOUN _____

VERB _____

ADJECTIVE _____

NUMBER _____

PLURAL NOUN _____

A PLACE _____

NOUN _____

NOUN _____

VERB ENDING IN "ING" _____

SILLY WORD _____

ADJECTIVE _____

PLURAL NOUN _____

TYPE OF FOOD _____

NOUN _____

PART OF THE BODY _____

PART OF THE BODY _____

MAD LIBS®
THE FIRST HOLIDAY IN FOREVER

Elsa and Anna were ready to celebrate! It was their first _____
ADJECTIVE

holiday together in a very long time. The sisters had spent many years

apart when they were young _____. Now that they were
PLURAL NOUN

grown, the girls were so excited they could hardly _____!
VERB

They were ready to eat, drink, and be _____! The once-lonely
ADJECTIVE

castle soon would be filled with _____ of their closest
NUMBER

_____ from all around (the) _____! Their frosty
PLURAL NOUN   A PLACE

friend, Olaf, was looking forward to the _____ party just as
NOUN

much as they were. The energetic little _____-man was
NOUN

_____ all around the castle, yelling "_____"
VERB ENDING IN "ING"   SILLY WORD

and getting in the way of the party preparations. He had never seen

so many festively _____ decorations, brightly wrapped
ADJECTIVE

_____, or delicious-looking _____-cakes. In fact,
PLURAL NOUN   TYPE OF FOOD

there were so many wonderful things to look at that Olaf's

_____ even fell off a few times. Luckily, Elsa and Anna were
NOUN

there to help him put his _____ back on his _____
PART OF THE BODY   PART OF THE BODY

where it belonged.

From OLAF'S FROZEN ADVENTURE MAD LIBS® • © 2017 Disney Enterprises, Inc.
Published by Mad Libs, an imprint of Penguin Random House LLC.

MAD LIBS® is fun to play with friends, but you can also play it by yourself! To begin with, DO NOT look at the story on the page below. Fill in the blanks on this page with the words called for. Then, using the words you have selected, fill in the blank spaces in the story.

Now you've created your own hilarious MAD LIBS® game!

CASTLE-DECORATING TIPS

NOUN _____

A PLACE _____

VERB _____

ADJECTIVE _____

CELEBRITY _____

NUMBER _____

NOUN _____

COLOR _____

PLURAL NOUN _____

VERB ENDING IN "ING" _____

ANIMAL _____

NOUN _____

ARTICLE OF CLOTHING (PLURAL) _____

ADJECTIVE _____

CELEBRITY (FEMALE) _____

PERSON IN ROOM _____

PART OF THE BODY (PLURAL) _____

MAD LIBS®

CASTLE-DECORATING TIPS

Do you want your castle to be the best-looking _____ in (the)
NOUN

_____ at the holidays? Do you hope guests will stop and
A PLACE

_____ at the awesomeness of your _____ displays?
VERB   ADJECTIVE

Do you secretly want to be the _____ of holiday decorating?
CELEBRITY

Just try these handy tips:

- Why have only one tree when you can have _____?
  NUMBER

  Place them down the hallways, on stairwells, even in the

  _____-room! Decorate them in fancy themes—for
  NOUN

  example, consider using all _____ _____
  COLOR   PLURAL NOUN

  or try anything in the shape of a/an _____
  VERB ENDING IN "ING"

  _____.
  ANIMAL

- Get your knights into the holiday spirit by replacing their armor

  with _____-themed _____.
  NOUN   ARTICLE OF CLOTHING (PLURAL)

- And don't forget about those _____ life-size portraits of
  ADJECTIVE

  King Agnarr, Queen _____, and _____
  CELEBRITY (FEMALE)   PERSON IN ROOM

  hanging in the hallway. String them with lights and watch their

  _____ twinkle!
  PART OF THE BODY (PLURAL)

MAD LIBS® is fun to play with friends, but you can also play it by yourself! To begin with, DO NOT look at the story on the page below. Fill in the blanks on this page with the words called for. Then, using the words you have selected, fill in the blank spaces in the story.

Now you've created your own hilarious MAD LIBS® game!

SEASONAL HELP WANTED

ADJECTIVE _____

PLURAL NOUN _____

VERB _____

CELEBRITY _____

ADJECTIVE _____

PART OF THE BODY (PLURAL) _____

VERB ENDING IN "ING" _____

NUMBER _____

PLURAL NOUN _____

COLOR _____

ARTICLE OF CLOTHING _____

NUMBER _____

TYPE OF FOOD _____

PART OF THE BODY _____

ADJECTIVE _____

VERB _____

MAD LIBS®

SEASONAL HELP WANTED

Are you hardworking, _____, and comfortable around royal
_____ ADJECTIVE
_____? Can you picture yourself going to a castle to
PLURAL NOUN
_____ every day from 8 a.m. to 5 p.m.? Do you have the
VERB
patience needed to deal with an energetic little snowman named

_____ who loves to give _____ hugs? If so, then *you*
CELEBRITY   ADJECTIVE
might be perfect for a position at Arendelle Castle, where the staff

could use an extra set of _____ to help with the
PART OF THE BODY (PLURAL)
busy holiday season. Although experience is not required, we prefer

candidates with sweeping, washing, and _____ skills.
VERB ENDING IN "ING"
Salary is _____ _____ per week, plus meals. You will
NUMBER   PLURAL NOUN
also be provided with an official castle uniform consisting of a/an

_____ _____. If the idea of sweeping the floors
COLOR   ARTICLE OF CLOTHING
of _____ rooms, stuffing endless trays of pastries with
NUMBER
_____ custard, searching for Olaf's _____
TYPE OF FOOD   PART OF THE BODY
whenever it goes missing, and performing other _____ duties
ADJECTIVE
as assigned appeals to you, then this job could be right for you.

_____ today for an application!
VERB

MAD LIBS® is fun to play with friends, but you can also play it by yourself! To begin with, DO NOT look at the story on the page below. Fill in the blanks on this page with the words called for. Then, using the words you have selected, fill in the blank spaces in the story.

Now you've created your own hilarious MAD LIBS® game!

HOLIDAY EATING

ADJECTIVE _____

NOUN _____

TYPE OF FOOD _____

TYPE OF LIQUID _____

SILLY WORD _____

NUMBER _____

PLURAL NOUN _____

PLURAL NOUN _____

ADJECTIVE _____

COLOR _____

NOUN _____

ADJECTIVE _____

PLURAL NOUN _____

TYPE OF FOOD _____

MAD LIBS®

HOLIDAY EATING

Since it's their first holiday in forever, Elsa and Anna have planned a

feast fit for a/an _____ king—or a royal _____! Here's
       ADJECTIVE   NOUN

what's on the menu:

- Party beverages, including _____ punch and hot
                                  TYPE OF FOOD

  _____ with marshmallows
    TYPE OF LIQUID

- A *kransekake*, also called "_____," which is a wreath
                              SILLY WORD

  cake made from _____ ring-shaped _____
               NUMBER   PLURAL NOUN

  stacked on top of each other

- Fruit salad with juicy _____, _____
                      PLURAL NOUN   ADJECTIVE

  _____ grapes, and _____-berries
      COLOR   NOUN

- Frosted _____ cookies shaped like snowflakes,
           ADJECTIVE

  snowmen, and—best of all—snow-_____
                               PLURAL NOUN

- Last but not least, snow cones topped with delicious

  _____-flavored syrup.
     TYPE OF FOOD

MAD LIBS® is fun to play with friends, but you can also play it by yourself! To begin with, DO NOT look at the story on the page below. Fill in the blanks on this page with the words called for. Then, using the words you have selected, fill in the blank spaces in the story.

Now you've created your own hilarious MAD LIBS® game!

ODE TO OLAF

ADJECTIVE _____

NOUN _____

PLURAL NOUN _____

CELEBRITY _____

A PLACE _____

COLOR _____

TYPE OF FOOD _____

ARTICLE OF CLOTHING (PLURAL) _____

ADJECTIVE _____

VERB _____

SILLY WORD _____

TYPE OF LIQUID _____

ADVERB _____

VERB ENDING IN "ING" _____

PART OF THE BODY _____

MAD LIBS®

ODE TO OLAF

Feeling _____ and in need of a hug? Then give Olaf a call!
 ADJECTIVE

Even though he's made of snow, he's the warmest _____ of all.
 NOUN

His very best _____ are Elsa and Anna; he likes
 PLURAL NOUN

_____ and Sven as well.
 CELEBRITY

He's the most popular snowman in (the) _____—or at least
 A PLACE

in Arendelle.

His nose is a long _____ _____ while his
 COLOR TYPE OF FOOD

_____ are made from coal.
 ARTICLE OF CLOTHING (PLURAL)

This funny, _____ snowman often has trouble staying whole!
 ADJECTIVE

Sometimes he'll _____ in a sauna and—_____!—
 VERB SILLY WORD

he'll melt without a care.

He becomes a puddle of _____ until he's tossed into
 TYPE OF LIQUID

_____ cold air!
 ADVERB

So when Olaf and his friends are _____ together, one
 VERB ENDING IN "ING"

thing is important to know . . .

Sometimes this excitable snowman's _____ will fall off his
 PART OF THE BODY

body and into the snow!

MAD LIBS® is fun to play with friends, but you can also play it by yourself! To begin with, DO NOT look at the story on the page below. Fill in the blanks on this page with the words called for. Then, using the words you have selected, fill in the blank spaces in the story.

Now you've created your own hilarious MAD LIBS® game!

THE HISTORY OF THE JULE BELL

NOUN _____

ADJECTIVE _____

CELEBRITY (MALE) _____

SILLY WORD _____

A PLACE _____

COLOR _____

NOUN _____

ADJECTIVE _____

ANIMAL _____

PLURAL NOUN _____

VERB ENDING IN "ING" _____

ADJECTIVE _____

ANIMAL (PLURAL) _____

PART OF THE BODY (PLURAL) _____

The ringing of the Jule Bell at noon signaled the beginning of the

_____ season each year in Arendelle. This had been a/an
NOUN

_____ tradition even before Queen Elsa's father, King
ADJECTIVE

_____, ruled the kingdom. "Jule" comes from the ancient
CELEBRITY (MALE)

word "_____" and refers to the holiday season in the lands of
SILLY WORD

the Far North such as Arendelle, the Southern Isles, and (the)

_____. The shiny _____ Jule Bell featured a large
A PLACE   COLOR

engraving of a bright _____ star in the center and bands of
NOUN

smaller _____ etchings symbolizing the spirit of the season.
ADJECTIVE

On the day of the ceremony, the Jule Bell was transported by a/an

_____-drawn sleigh to the palace courtyard, where it was
ANIMAL

hung in the bell tower, and all the _____ of Arendelle
PLURAL NOUN

gathered to welcome the holidays with merry singing and

_____. Hearing the ancient Jule Bell chime was a/an
VERB ENDING IN "ING"

_____ experience—like listening to a joyful chorus of
ADJECTIVE

_____. For the citizens of Arendelle, it was truly music
ANIMAL (PLURAL)

to their _____!
PART OF THE BODY (PLURAL)

From OLAF'S FROZEN ADVENTURE MAD LIBS® • © 2017 Disney Enterprises, Inc.
Published by Mad Libs, an imprint of Penguin Random House LLC.

MAD LIBS® is fun to play with friends, but you can also play it by yourself! To begin with, DO NOT look at the story on the page below. Fill in the blanks on this page with the words called for. Then, using the words you have selected, fill in the blank spaces in the story.

Now you've created your own hilarious MAD LIBS® game!

FLEMMY THE FUNGUS TROLL

PLURAL NOUN _____

ADJECTIVE _____

VERB _____

ADJECTIVE _____

CELEBRITY _____

ANIMAL _____

NOUN _____

ADJECTIVE _____

SILLY WORD _____

PLURAL NOUN _____

PART OF THE BODY _____

TYPE OF LIQUID _____

NOUN _____

NOUN _____

PERSON IN ROOM _____

The trolls were a close-knit group of _____ and the only
_{PLURAL NOUN}

family that Kristoff had ever really known. Growing up among the

_____ trolls was so much fun, especially at the holidays. It was
ADJECTIVE

tradition to _____ together while singing "The Ballad of
VERB

Flemmingrad," a tale about a/an _____, mushroom-covered
ADJECTIVE

troll who made all your holiday wishes come true! Flemmy, as he was

called, took wishing to a troll new level! If you wanted a/an

_____ straw doll or a sweet little pet _____, Flemmy
CELEBRITY ANIMAL

was the _____ to summon! All you had to do was lick his
NOUN

smelly, _____ forehead, make your holiday wish, and—
ADJECTIVE

_____—it would come true! Yes, Flemmy might have dirt
SILLY WORD

caked all over his _____ and moss growing out of his
PLURAL NOUN

_____, and he may ooze muddy _____ all over
PART OF THE BODY TYPE OF LIQUID

your _____. But the season wouldn't be the same without
NOUN

him. After all, nothing says the holidays like a muddy, moldy

_____ named _____.
NOUN PERSON IN ROOM

From OLAF'S FROZEN ADVENTURE MAD LIBS® • © 2017 Disney Enterprises, Inc.
Published by Mad Libs, an imprint of Penguin Random House LLC.

MAD LIBS® is fun to play with friends, but you can also play it by yourself! To begin with, DO NOT look at the story on the page below. Fill in the blanks on this page with the words called for. Then, using the words you have selected, fill in the blank spaces in the story.

Now you've created your own hilarious MAD LIBS® game!

A VERY KRISTOFF HOLIDAY

ADJECTIVE _____

PART OF THE BODY _____

VERB (PAST TENSE) _____

PLURAL NOUN _____

NOUN _____

ADJECTIVE _____

A PLACE _____

ANIMAL _____

NUMBER _____

COLOR _____

NOUN _____

PERSON IN ROOM _____

CELEBRITY _____

NOUN _____

TYPE OF LIQUID _____

TYPE OF FOOD (PLURAL) _____

ADJECTIVE _____

MAD LIBS®

A VERY KRISTOFF HOLIDAY

Since it was his first holiday with Anna, Kristoff wanted to make it

extra-_____ so it would always hold a special place in Anna's
　　　　　ADJECTIVE

_____. Kristoff _____ long and hard,
PART OF THE BODY　　　　VERB (PAST TENSE)

wondering what he could do. He would have to do something that

didn't cost a lot of _____. After all, he was just a common
　　　　　　　　PLURAL NOUN

_____, while Anna was a princess. Luckily, she was easygoing
　　NOUN

and _____. Kristoff thought about taking her for a moonlit
　　ADJECTIVE

ride through the frosty forest of (the) _____ in his
　　　　　　　　　　　　A PLACE

_____-drawn sleigh. He considered making her a bouquet of
ANIMAL

_____ long-stemmed _____ _____-flowers
NUMBER　　　　　　COLOR　　　　NOUN

from ice. Serenading her with his music-loving troll friends,

_____ and _____, was another option. Or he could
PERSON IN ROOM　　　CELEBRITY

prepare a romantic dinner complete with _____ stew, chilled
　　　　　　　　　　　　　　NOUN

_____, and _____ roasted over an open
TYPE OF LIQUID　　　TYPE OF FOOD (PLURAL)

fire. Whatever he decided to do, Kristoff hoped Anna would love it!

He wanted her holiday to be downright _____!
　　　　　　　　　　　ADJECTIVE

From OLAF'S FROZEN ADVENTURE MAD LIBS® • © 2017 Disney Enterprises, Inc.
Published by Mad Libs, an imprint of Penguin Random House LLC.

MAD LIBS® is fun to play with friends, but you can also play it by yourself! To begin with, DO NOT look at the story on the page below. Fill in the blanks on this page with the words called for. Then, using the words you have selected, fill in the blank spaces in the story.

Now you've created your own hilarious MAD LIBS® game!

SLEIGH MAINTENANCE

VERB ENDING IN "ING" _____

ADJECTIVE _____

PLURAL NOUN _____

ADJECTIVE _____

VERB _____

PART OF THE BODY _____

NOUN _____

ANIMAL _____

TYPE OF LIQUID _____

TYPE OF FOOD (PLURAL) _____

TYPE OF LIQUID _____

NOUN _____

ADJECTIVE _____

PERSON IN ROOM _____

NOUN _____

MAD LIBS

SLEIGH MAINTENANCE

Whether you're dashing through the snow or _____ in
<u>VERB ENDING IN "ING"</u>

it, a slick sled is required. Keep your sleigh in _____ working
<u>ADJECTIVE</u>

order with these easy care tips:

1. Tighten all the nuts, bolts, and _____.
   <u>PLURAL NOUN</u>

2. Sharpen the _____ blades to help the sleigh
   <u>ADJECTIVE</u>

   _____ better in the snow.
   <u>VERB</u>

3. Make sure the harness is securely attached and won't slip off

   the _____ of the _____ pulling the sleigh.
   <u>PART OF THE BODY</u>   <u>NOUN</u>

4. Give the lead _____ enough _____ to drink and
   <u>ANIMAL</u>   <u>TYPE OF LIQUID</u>

   plenty of _____ to keep up his energy.
   <u>TYPE OF FOOD (PLURAL)</u>

5. Polish the sled with a/an _____-based wood
   <u>TYPE OF LIQUID</u>

   finisher so it gleams like a shiny new _____!
   <u>NOUN</u>

6. Most importantly, don't let _____, inexperienced
   <u>ADJECTIVE</u>

   drivers like Olaf or _____ drive the sleigh, or it might
   <u>PERSON IN ROOM</u>

   plunge off a cliff and burst into a fiery _____!
   <u>NOUN</u>

From OLAF'S FROZEN ADVENTURE MAD LIBS® • © 2017 Disney Enterprises, Inc.
Published by Mad Libs, an imprint of Penguin Random House LLC.

MAD LIBS® is fun to play with friends, but you can also play it by yourself! To begin with, DO NOT look at the story on the page below. Fill in the blanks on this page with the words called for. Then, using the words you have selected, fill in the blank spaces in the story.

Now you've created your own hilarious MAD LIBS® game!

HITTING THE TRAIL

ADJECTIVE _____

PLURAL NOUN _____

PART OF THE BODY (PLURAL) _____

PERSON IN ROOM (FEMALE) _____

PLURAL NOUN _____

ANIMAL _____

A PLACE _____

NOUN _____

VERB (PAST TENSE) _____

PART OF THE BODY _____

ADJECTIVE _____

NOUN _____

SILLY WORD _____

VERB _____

ADJECTIVE _____

VERB _____

It made Olaf's heart break to see poor Elsa and Anna looking so

_____. The sisters were the only _____ in
　　　ADJECTIVE　　　　　　　　　　　　　　　　　PLURAL NOUN

Arendelle who didn't have any holiday traditions to celebrate. Olaf

wondered what he could do to put smiles back on their

_____. After all, Elsa and _____
PART OF THE BODY (PLURAL)　　　　　　　　　PERSON IN ROOM (FEMALE)

were his very dearest _____! Olaf suggested to Kristoff's
　　　　　　　　　　　PLURAL NOUN

pet _____, Sven, that they travel around (the) _____
　　　ANIMAL　　　　　　　　　　　　　　　　　　　　　A PLACE

and visit every _____ in the entire kingdom to ask how they
　　　　　　　　NOUN

_____ at the holidays. Then they could pile those
VERB (PAST TENSE)

traditions into the sleigh and bring them home to Elsa and Anna. Sven

nodded his _____—that was a/an _____ plan! So
　　　PART OF THE BODY　　　　　　　　　ADJECTIVE

Olaf hitched Sven to the _____ and—_____—off
　　　　　　　　　　　　NOUN　　　　　　　SILLY WORD

they went! Olaf and Sven to the rescue! The little snowman was

determined not to rest or _____ until he had found a way to
　　　　　　　　　　　　VERB

make the holidays _____ for his family. He and Sven were
　　　　　　　　　ADJECTIVE

either going to find the traditions needed to save the season—or

_____ trying!
　VERB

MAD LIBS® is fun to play with friends, but you can also play it by yourself! To begin with, DO NOT look at the story on the page below. Fill in the blanks on this page with the words called for. Then, using the words you have selected, fill in the blank spaces in the story.

Now you've created your own hilarious MAD LIBS® game!

ARENDELLE TRADITIONS

ADJECTIVE _____

NOUN _____

A PLACE _____

VERB ENDING IN "ING" _____

SILLY WORD _____

TYPE OF FOOD _____

TYPE OF FOOD _____

NOUN _____

SILLY WORD _____

NUMBER _____

PART OF THE BODY _____

NOUN _____

PLURAL NOUN _____

ADJECTIVE _____

ANIMAL _____

NOUN _____

PLURAL NOUN _____

MAD LIBS

ARENDELLE TRADITIONS

The holidays in Arendelle were a joyous, _____ time of year!
ADJECTIVE

Every _____ had its own ways of celebrating, and Olaf and
NOUN

Sven learned a lot about traditions as they traveled around (the)

_____ visiting families. For example, it was common to spend
A PLACE

hours in the kitchen, cooking and baking and _____.
VERB ENDING IN "ING"

A popular dessert to make was "_____-*kake*," which
SILLY WORD

meant "_____ cake." It was covered with creamy
TYPE OF FOOD

_____ frosting and topped with ripe _____-berries.
TYPE OF FOOD   NOUN

Also, many families had a *tomte* (or "_____") in their home.
SILLY WORD

This mythical creature was typically only _____ feet tall, had a
NUMBER

long beard on his _____, and wore a pointy _____
PART OF THE BODY   NOUN

on his head—just like an elf. Legend said the *tomte* came to the front

doors of houses to leave _____ for those children who had
PLURAL NOUN

been _____ all year. The *tomte* was accompanied by a
ADJECTIVE

straw _____ known as the "Jule _____." No
ANIMAL   NOUN

matter the traditions, the holidays were always celebrated with family

and _____.
PLURAL NOUN

MAD LIBS® is fun to play with friends, but you can also play it by yourself! To begin with, DO NOT look at the story on the page below. Fill in the blanks on this page with the words called for. Then, using the words you have selected, fill in the blank spaces in the story.

Now you've created your own hilarious MAD LIBS® game!

HAPPY HOO-LIDAYS
FROM OAKEN

NOUN _____

NUMBER _____

NOUN _____

ADJECTIVE _____

ADJECTIVE _____

EXCLAMATION _____

PLURAL NOUN _____

NOUN _____

VERB ENDING IN "ING" _____

NOUN _____

VERB (PAST TENSE) _____

PART OF THE BODY _____

ARTICLE OF CLOTHING _____

TYPE OF LIQUID _____

ADJECTIVE _____

NOUN _____

NOUN _____

PART OF THE BODY (PLURAL) _____

MAD LIBS
HAPPY HOO-LIDAYS
FROM OAKEN

Yoo-hoo! Oaken here, proprietor of the local _____ Post and
NOUN

Sauna! The holidays are a busy time at my shop. Today, we had at least

_____ shoppers browsing our popular _____
NUMBER   NOUN

department and our _____ clearance section. It was a/an
                    ADJECTIVE

_____ holiday blowout! _____, why do
ADJECTIVE   EXCLAMATION

_____ always wait until the very last minute to shop?
PLURAL NOUN

Anyhoo, once the last _____ had finally left the store, my
                      NOUN

family and I were enjoying our old tradition of sweating and

_____ in the sauna when there was a knock at the
VERB ENDING IN "ING"

front _____. A magical snowman _____
      NOUN   VERB (PAST TENSE)

right there on my front porch. I invited him to come in out of the cold

and join us. He removed the coals from his _____, and I
                                            PART OF THE BODY

gave him his own miniature _____ to wear. Soon the
                           ARTICLE OF CLOTHING

little fellow started to melt into a puddle of _____. So I
                                              TYPE OF LIQUID

did what any _____ host would do—I scooped him up in a/an
             ADJECTIVE

_____ and tossed him outside. Luckily, he turned into a frozen
NOUN

_____ again right before my very _____.
NOUN   PART OF THE BODY (PLURAL)

From OLAF'S FROZEN ADVENTURE MAD LIBS® • © 2017 Disney Enterprises, Inc.
Published by Mad Libs, an imprint of Penguin Random House LLC.

MAD LIBS® is fun to play with friends, but you can also play it by yourself! To begin with, DO NOT look at the story on the page below. Fill in the blanks on this page with the words called for. Then, using the words you have selected, fill in the blank spaces in the story.

Now you've created your own hilarious MAD LIBS® game!

DO YOU WANT TO MELT A SNOWMAN?

PLURAL NOUN _____

NOUN _____

ADJECTIVE _____

PART OF THE BODY (PLURAL) _____

NOUN _____

TYPE OF FOOD _____

ADJECTIVE _____

TYPE OF FOOD _____

A PLACE _____

VERB ENDING IN "ING" _____

PLURAL NOUN _____

NOUN _____

ADJECTIVE _____

NUMBER _____

NOUN _____

PART OF THE BODY _____

Olaf might like warm hugs, but warm _____ do not like
PLURAL NOUN

him! The best way for the cheerful little _____-man to beat
NOUN

the _____ heat is to avoid any of these activities:
ADJECTIVE

- Putting a pair of oven mitts on his _____
  PART OF THE BODY (PLURAL)

  and reaching into a hot _____ to pull out a delicious
  NOUN

  _____ pie baked to perfection
  TYPE OF FOOD

- Taking a/an _____ bubble bath—especially when
  ADJECTIVE

  surrounded by a bunch of burning _____-scented
  TYPE OF FOOD

  candles

- Going camping in the woods near (the) _____ and
  A PLACE

  _____ too close to a roaring fire made from
  VERB ENDING IN "ING"

  wood and dried _____
  PLURAL NOUN

- Cruising on a huge _____-ship to a tropical island paradise
  NOUN

  where the _____ temperatures reach _____ degrees
  ADJECTIVE NUMBER

- Running a marathon or engaging in any sort of physical

  _____, because Olaf wouldn't just lose weight—he'd
  NOUN

  lose his entire _____!
  PART OF THE BODY

MAD LIBS® is fun to play with friends, but you can also play it by yourself! To begin with, DO NOT look at the story on the page below. Fill in the blanks on this page with the words called for. Then, using the words you have selected, fill in the blank spaces in the story.

Now you've created your own hilarious MAD LIBS® game!

DASHING THROUGH THE SNOW

ADJECTIVE _____

A PLACE _____

NOUN _____

ADJECTIVE _____

NOUN _____

ANIMAL _____

CELEBRITY _____

A PLACE _____

VERB ENDING IN "ING" _____

NOUN _____

NUMBER _____

PLURAL NOUN _____

COLOR _____

ADJECTIVE _____

ADVERB _____

ADJECTIVE _____

MAD LIBS
DASHING THROUGH
THE SNOW

Something _____ is unfolding in the forest on the outskirts of
　　　　　　 ADJECTIVE

(the) _____ . It seems that a runaway _____ packed with
　　　 A PLACE　　　　　　　　　　　　　　　　 NOUN

holiday traditions is headed for _____ disaster! Here's what
　　　　　　　　　　　　　　　　 ADJECTIVE

we currently know: A determined little _____ named Olaf
　　　　　　　　　　　　　　　　　 NOUN

and his faithful furry _____ companion, _____,
　　　　　　　　　 ANIMAL　　　　　　　　　　 CELEBRITY

spent hours today scouring (the) _____ for traditions worthy
　　　　　　　　　　　　　　　 A PLACE

of their beloved Queen Elsa and Princess Anna. As they were dashing

through the snow, _____ all the way, the overloaded
　　　　　　　 VERB ENDING IN "ING"

sleigh broke free and plunged over a/an _____ cliff,
　　　　　　　　　　　　　　　　　　　　 NOUN

plummeting _____ feet to some dangerously sharp
　　　　　　 NUMBER

_____ below. The sleigh exploded in a massive blast of
PLURAL NOUN

bright _____ sparks. Things are not looking _____
　　　 COLOR　　　　　　　　　　　　　　　　　　　　 ADJECTIVE

for our heroes at this moment. Can the holidays be saved in time?

Everyone is _____ waiting to see what will happen as this
　　　　　　 ADVERB

_____ situation unfolds!
ADJECTIVE

MAD LIBS® is fun to play with friends, but you can also play it by yourself! To begin with, DO NOT look at the story on the page below. Fill in the blanks on this page with the words called for. Then, using the words you have selected, fill in the blank spaces in the story.

Now you've created your own hilarious MAD LIBS® game!

FLEMMY STEW RECIPE

VERB ENDING IN "ING" _____

PART OF THE BODY _____

NOUN _____

EXCLAMATION _____

ADJECTIVE _____

PERSON IN ROOM (FEMALE) _____

NOUN _____

CELEBRITY _____

PLURAL NOUN _____

NUMBER _____

TYPE OF LIQUID _____

ANIMAL _____

PLURAL NOUN _____

VERB _____

ADJECTIVE _____

TYPE OF FOOD _____

ADJECTIVE _____

NOUN _____

MAD LIBS

FLEMMY STEW RECIPE

Kristoff was busy _____ over a hot stove. He leaned
                    VERB ENDING IN "ING"

his _____ over a simmering _____ and inhaled
    PART OF THE BODY   NOUN

deeply. _____! It smelled deliciously _____!
         EXCLAMATION   ADJECTIVE

Kristoff wanted to surprise Anna and _____ with a
                                      PERSON IN ROOM (FEMALE)

holiday meal of Flemmy Stew—a traditional _____ favorite
                                            NOUN

within the troll community. Named after the holiday-wish-granting

troll, _____, Flemmy Stew is a simple mixture of hearty
        CELEBRITY

vegetables and flavorful _____. Whipping up this
                          PLURAL NOUN

popular stew is easy! Just start by boiling _____ cups of
                                             NUMBER

_____. Next, add mushrooms, carrots, _____-worms,
TYPE OF LIQUID   ANIMAL

and any other _____ that live, grow, or _____ in
               PLURAL NOUN   VERB

the dirt. Then, toss in a couple pounds of _____ rocks for a
                                            ADJECTIVE

crunchy texture. Season to taste with salt, pepper, and finely ground

_____. Let it simmer on "_____" for an hour. Once
TYPE OF FOOD   ADJECTIVE

you try the famous Flemmy Stew, you'll never want to go back to

regular old _____ Stew.
             NOUN

MAD LIBS® is fun to play with friends, but you can also play it by yourself! To begin with, DO NOT look at the story on the page below. Fill in the blanks on this page with the words called for. Then, using the words you have selected, fill in the blank spaces in the story.

Now you've created your own hilarious MAD LIBS® game!

INTO THE FOREST

A PLACE _____

VERB _____

NOUN _____

ADJECTIVE _____

SILLY WORD _____

NOUN _____

PART OF THE BODY (PLURAL) _____

ANIMAL (PLURAL) _____

ADJECTIVE _____

VERB ENDING IN "ING" _____

NOUN _____

CELEBRITY _____

ADJECTIVE _____

PLURAL NOUN _____

TYPE OF FOOD _____

NOUN _____

ADJECTIVE _____

Olaf was alone in the forest. He was trying to find his way home to

(the) _____ but didn't know which way to _____. It
     A PLACE   VERB

was getting late, and the _____ overhead was growing darker.
                                NOUN

The little snowman was surrounded by strange, _____
                                                    ADJECTIVE

sounds—like "OWOOOOOO" and "WHOOOOOOSH" and

"_____." And he saw small, _____-shaped lights
   SILLY WORD   NOUN

blinking at him from behind the tree branches. Were those the

_____ of wild _____? Olaf wondered if
PART OF THE BODY (PLURAL)   ANIMAL (PLURAL)

they liked warm, _____ hugs. He hurried through the forest,
                    ADJECTIVE

hoping that if he kept _____ hard enough, he would
                        VERB ENDING IN "ING"

find a way out of the wooded _____. Or maybe Elsa and Anna
                                NOUN

would form a search party with Kristoff and Sven and _____ to
                                                          CELEBRITY

come look for him. But Olaf was so disappointed that he had failed

his _____ mission of finding holiday traditions for his
        ADJECTIVE

two best _____. The only thing he had was a/an
            PLURAL NOUN

_____-filled fruitcake—and no _____ likes fruitcake!
TYPE OF FOOD   NOUN

This was not the _____ ending Olaf had been hoping for!
                     ADJECTIVE

From OLAF'S FROZEN ADVENTURE MAD LIBS® • © 2017 Disney Enterprises, Inc.
Published by Mad Libs, an imprint of Penguin Random House LLC.

MAD LIBS® is fun to play with friends, but you can also play it by yourself! To begin with, DO NOT look at the story on the page below. Fill in the blanks on this page with the words called for. Then, using the words you have selected, fill in the blank spaces in the story.

Now you've created your own hilarious MAD LIBS® game!

A TRUNKFUL OF MEMORIES

VERB (PAST TENSE) _____

ADJECTIVE _____

PLURAL NOUN _____

ADJECTIVE _____

PLURAL NOUN _____

VERB ENDING IN "ING" _____

ANIMAL _____

NOUN _____

NOUN _____

ARTICLE OF CLOTHING _____

COLOR _____

NOUN _____

CELEBRITY (MALE) _____

ARTICLE OF CLOTHING (PLURAL) _____

PART OF THE BODY (PLURAL) _____

NUMBER _____

NOUN _____

ADJECTIVE _____

MAD LIBS®

A TRUNKFUL OF MEMORIES

No matter how hard she _____, Anna could not recall
                    VERB (PAST TENSE)

any _____ holiday traditions that her family had. So she went
     ADJECTIVE

to the castle's attic and rummaged through a trunk full of childhood

_____ to help her remember. She found _____
PLURAL NOUN   ADJECTIVE

costumes and other dress-up _____ that she would wear
                           PLURAL NOUN

when she pretended to be a/an _____ Viking, a
                       VERB ENDING IN "ING"

fire-breathing _____, or a/an _____ in shining
           ANIMAL   NOUN

armor. She found the _____ skates she used to zip around the
                   NOUN

castle. She found the sparkly _____ that she wore to her
                       ARTICLE OF CLOTHING

very first ball. She found Elsa's _____ stuffed _____,
                        COLOR   NOUN

Mr. _____. And she found lots and lots of the
     CELEBRITY (MALE)

_____ that Elsa had to wear on her
ARTICLE OF CLOTHING (PLURAL)

_____—there were at least _____ pairs!
PART OF THE BODY (PLURAL)   NUMBER

She didn't find anything that reminded her of the holidays when she

was a little _____. But the good thing about memories is that
         NOUN

you can always make new ones—and Anna was determined to make

them _____!
   ADJECTIVE

From OLAF'S FROZEN ADVENTURE MAD LIBS® • © 2017 Disney Enterprises, Inc.
Published by Mad Libs, an imprint of Penguin Random House LLC.

MAD LIBS® is fun to play with friends, but you can also play it by yourself! To begin with, DO NOT look at the story on the page below. Fill in the blanks on this page with the words called for. Then, using the words you have selected, fill in the blank spaces in the story.

Now you've created your own hilarious MAD LIBS® game!

IT WAS ALWAYS OLAF

VERB ENDING IN "ING" _____

NOUN _____

ADJECTIVE _____

PLURAL NOUN _____

ADJECTIVE _____

NOUN _____

NOUN _____

PART OF THE BODY _____

SILLY WORD _____

PLURAL NOUN _____

TYPE OF FOOD _____

VERB ENDING IN "ING" _____

TYPE OF LIQUID _____

PLURAL NOUN _____

ADJECTIVE _____

CELEBRITY (MALE) _____

MAD LIBS®

IT WAS ALWAYS OLAF

Growing up, Anna spent a lot of time _____ by herself in
VERB ENDING IN "ING"

the castle. That's because her older _____, Elsa, usually locked
NOUN

herself away in her room. It was a/an _____, lonely life for
ADJECTIVE

both girls. One day, many _____ later, the sisters found
PLURAL NOUN

_____ drawings that Anna had done as a young _____.
ADJECTIVE   NOUN

In one drawing, the sisters were building a snow-_____.
NOUN

Elsa was waving her _____—and, _____—Olaf
PART OF THE BODY   SILLY WORD

had appeared! Anna was holding two _____ for his eyes
PLURAL NOUN

and a long, slender _____ for his nose. Another drawing
TYPE OF FOOD

showed Olaf and the girls ice-_____ in the ballroom
VERB ENDING IN "ING"

on a large rink made from frozen _____. In yet another
TYPE OF LIQUID

drawing, Anna and Elsa were sitting on Olaf and sledding along

mounds of fresh, snowy _____. That's when the girls
PLURAL NOUN

realized that they *did* have a childhood tradition that kept them

_____ even when they were apart—it was a little snowman
ADJECTIVE

named _____!
CELEBRITY (MALE)

From OLAF'S FROZEN ADVENTURE MAD LIBS® • © 2017 Disney Enterprises, Inc.
Published by Mad Libs, an imprint of Penguin Random House LLC.

MAD LIBS® is fun to play with friends, but you can also play it by yourself! To begin with, DO NOT look at the story on the page below. Fill in the blanks on this page with the words called for. Then, using the words you have selected, fill in the blank spaces in the story.

Now you've created your own hilarious MAD LIBS® game!

A KINGDOM CELEBRATES

VERB ENDING IN "ING" _____

ANIMAL (PLURAL) _____

PART OF THE BODY _____

ADJECTIVE _____

NUMBER _____

TYPE OF FOOD _____

ADJECTIVE _____

A PLACE _____

PLURAL NOUN _____

PERSON IN ROOM _____

NOUN _____

PLURAL NOUN _____

TYPE OF FOOD (PLURAL) _____

VERB ENDING IN "ING" _____

NOUN _____

NOUN _____

MAD LIBS®

A KINGDOM CELEBRATES

After _____ for his life through the dark forest with a

VERB ENDING IN "ING"

pack of wild _____ on his heels, Olaf was found by his

ANIMAL (PLURAL)

friends stuck _____-first in a snowbank. Elsa and Anna

PART OF THE BODY

were so relieved to find their friend safe and _____ that they

ADJECTIVE

gave him _____ warm hugs, and Sven licked him so hard that

NUMBER

Olaf's _____ nose came off! As long as they were together, the

TYPE OF FOOD

holidays would be happy and _____ after all. Suddenly, people

ADJECTIVE

from all over (the) _____ spilled into the forest clearing

A PLACE

carrying pretty lighted _____ to hang in the trees. Then,

PLURAL NOUN

_____ and the other members of the royal _____ staff

PERSON IN ROOM   NOUN

appeared with the smoked _____ and the spiral-sliced

PLURAL NOUN

_____ and the rest of the delicious food from the

TYPE OF FOOD (PLURAL)

holiday gathering back at the castle. The royal holiday party was back

on! People were laughing, feasting, and _____ under the

VERB ENDING IN "ING"

star-filled _____. Thanks to Olaf, it would be a merry and

NOUN

memorable _____ after all!

NOUN

From OLAF'S FROZEN ADVENTURE MAD LIBS® • © 2017 Disney Enterprises, Inc.
Published by Mad Libs, an imprint of Penguin Random House LLC.